Digital Manufacturing FOR DUMMIES®

A Wiley Brand

Proto Labs® Special Edition

by Brian Underdahl

FOR DUMMIES®

A Wiley Brand

Digital Manufacturing For Dummies®, Proto Labs® Special Edition

Published by
John Wiley & Sons, Inc.
111 River St.
Hoboken, NJ 07030-5774
www.wiley.com

Publisher's Acknowledgments

Some of the people who helped bring this book to market include the following:

Project Editor: Carrie A. Johnson

Acquisitions Editor: Katie Mohr

Editorial Manager: Rev Mengle

Business Development Representative: Kimberley Schumacker

Production Editor: Suresh Srinivasan

Table of Contents

Introduction

● ●

Digital manufacturing encompasses several different processes that serve different needs during the product life cycle. You may need a quick prototype that shows the general appearance of a product in order to validate its concept. Or, you may need a high-quality prototype in order to test the functionality of your design. Once you've validated the concept and verified the form, fit, and function of your part, you may move into low-volume production or need bridge tooling while a full-scale production mold is being made. Short-run manufacturing is frequently used to produce up to 10,000 parts in both cases. Regardless of what stage you're in, digital manufacturing can be used to deliver products to market faster and more cost-effectively and maintain them throughout the duration of their product life cycle.

About This Book

Are you trying to figure out how to quickly get the parts you need for prototype testing or low-volume production? If so, this book is designed to help. *Digital Manufacturing For Dummies,* Proto Labs Special Edition, examines the various 3-D printing, CNC machining, and injection molding technologies used in digital manufacturing and how to leverage each process to bring products to market faster. You also discover what you need to know as you evaluate vendors and processes to solve your need for quick-turnaround product development and production. Along the way, you see how these technologies fill different needs and how they compare in important areas.

Foolish Assumptions

Engineering departments and even private individuals now have ready access to design tools that are light-years ahead of what was available a decade ago. Being able to develop a three-dimensional model using CAD software can help you better visualize the part and evaluate what needs to be included in the design. As I am writing this book, I assume that you have access to design tools like these, have an existing design that you want to produce, and don't have the capability to do the manufacturing yourself.

Icons Used in This Book

This book uses the following icons to call your attention to information you may find helpful in particular ways.

 The information marked by this icon is important and therefore repeated for emphasis. This way, you can easily spot noteworthy information when you refer to the book later.

 This icon points out extra-helpful information.

 This icon marks places where technical matters, such as jargon and whatnot, are discussed. Sorry, it can't be helped, but it's intended to be helpful.

 Paragraphs marked with this icon call attention to common pitfalls that you may encounter.

Chapter 1

Understanding the Importance of Digital Manufacturing

● ●

In This Chapter

▶ Getting the product life cycle started

▶ Understanding the development process

▶ Using the appropriate process

▶ Getting to market quickly

▶ Transitioning from prototype to product

▶ Looking at the rest of the product life cycle

● ●

*D*igital manufacturing is technology-enabled manufacturing that uses computing power to transform traditional and modern manufacturing methods into more efficient processes. The result of digital manufacturing is higher productivity, faster cycle times, less waste, and significant cost savings. This chapter provides an introduction to digital manufacturing, shows you the different stages involved, and helps you understand what you need to know to get started. You also see why your project may involve more than one process as it moves from prototype to market.

Looking at Early Stages of the Product Life Cycle

The prospect of developing a new product and bringing it to market can be very exciting. Although you can follow more than one path, several stages typically apply, especially when digital manufacturing capabilities are available.

First, of course, you need to have an idea for a product that you want to introduce. At this point, it doesn't matter if you are an individual inventor or someone working for a large company. What's important is that you can visualize a physical product that you feel will be worth the time and effort necessary to bring it to market. Armed with your product idea, it's time to move on to the next stage.

Concept models

Most commonly, product development begins with drawings or computer models that represent the product. Computer models are typically quick to make and can be used for certain types of analysis. After the basic idea is captured, it's time for a physical model that demonstrates the concept of the product. This model often is nonfunctional, but it gives a general impression of what the finished product may look like.

Concept models allow you to assess feedback from within your company as well as conduct a preliminary market analysis to gauge whether the product is appealing to consumers. Concept models work well because most people find it far easier to comprehend an actual physical object than they do an abstract idea. If internal company feedback and market analysis produce positive results, you'll likely move to the next step in the production process.

Testing form, fit, and functionality

Although a concept model can provide a general idea of what your finished product will look like, it probably won't be something that people would actually buy. To get closer to that goal, you need to expend a little more effort toward creating something with the form, fit, and functionality of a finished product.

To begin, you need to develop a 3-D computer aided design (CAD) model of the product and its components. This digital model is what the manufacturer uses to produce the parts that make up your product.

You want to choose a manufacturer that has the capability to perform an engineering analysis on your computer model to determine if the parts can actually be manufactured as designed and to suggest the best manufacturing options to suit your needs. For example, should the part be built up layer by layer, or would it be more appropriate to start with a solid block of material and cut away the excess? Identifying the right manufacturing process involves part geometry, volume, material used, cost, urgency, and several other important considerations.

It may take a couple of iterations before you're happy with every piece of your finished product, but that's the whole point of this stage of the product life cycle. You wouldn't want to put a product into actual production and then discover a major design flaw.

Low-volume production

After you've completed your initial testing, you may be ready to begin low-volume production. Even products that may become mass-market items often start with low-volume production in order to bring the product to market more quickly.

Companies with expertise in digital manufacturing may well be your best choice for low-volume production because they can offer the fast turnaround you need to beat competitors to market. In fact, depending on the manufacturer's capabilities, a digital manufacturing company may be able to meet the entire volume demanded, especially for niche market products.

Using Iterative Development and Pivoting

Very few products are perfect in their first iteration. More likely, you may find that you go through several designs as you work through flaws or other areas that need improvement. Obviously, manufacturing beginning with fairly small quantities of product make it much easier for you to engage in this iterative development process.

 Quick-turn digital manufacturing is lower cost and more flexible than traditional high-volume manufacturing. Part of its power is permitting multiple iterations fast. When is anything right on the first try?

Another common element in the product development process is discovering that a product may be used in unanticipated ways. These new uses may result in a pivot to a different way of thinking about how the product should be manufactured and marketed. For example, you may find unexpected demand for your product in a market with slightly different requirements, causing you to change materials or design.

Shifting between Processes

Digital manufacturing isn't a single process that uses one type of material. Instead, several different processes and materials may be appropriate during different stages of development and production. You might, for example, have the manufacturer create very early parts that provide the general look and feel of the product using a process and materials that wouldn't work for a finished product. But because these early parts might be inexpensive and quick to produce, it's easy for you to go through several iterations until you're satisfied with the form, fit, and appearance.

Later chapters in this book go into more depth on the processes and materials used in digital manufacturing, but basically some parts are suited to an additive process where the part is built up with layers of material, and other parts are best suited to a subtractive process that starts with a solid block of material that is machined into its final form. Yet other parts may only ever use a process like injection molding. Materials can range from low-strength plastics to extremely high-strength metals, depending on product needs.

Your digital manufacturing partner can discuss with you the best processes and materials to use at each stage of product development and production. But for your reference, check out Figure 1-1 for all the digital manufacturing process attributes.

	ADDITIVE MANUFACTURING						
Attribute	BJET	SL	FDM	PJET	SLS	DLP	DMLS
Quantity	POOR	POOR	POOR	POOR	POOR	POOR	POOR
Complexity	GOOD	GOOD	GOOD	GOOD	GOOD	GOOD	GOOD
Surface Finish	POOR	FAIR	POOR	FAIR	POOR	FAIR	POOR
Material Selection	POOR	FAIR	POOR	POOR	POOR	POOR	FAIR
Material Stability	FAIR	POOR	GOOD	POOR	FAIR	POOR	GOOD
Color	GOOD	POOR	FAIR	POOR	POOR	POOR	POOR
Tolerance	POOR	GOOD	POOR	POOR	FAIR	FAIR	FAIR
Speed	GOOD	GOOD	FAIR	GOOD	GOOD	GOOD	FAIR
Price (Low Volume)	GOOD	GOOD	GOOD	GOOD	GOOD	GOOD	GOOD
Price (High Volume)	POOR	POOR	POOR	POOR	POOR	POOR	POOR

	MACHINING	INJECTION MOLDING				
Attribute	CNC	IM	LSR	MIM	DIE CAST	THIXO
Quantity	FAIR	GOOD	GOOD	GOOD	GOOD	GOOD
Complexity	FAIR	GOOD	GOOD	GOOD	GOOD	GOOD
Surface Finish	GOOD	GOOD	GOOD	GOOD	GOOD	GOOD
Material Selection	GOOD	GOOD	GOOD	POOR	POOR	POOR
Material Stability	GOOD	GOOD	GOOD	GOOD	GOOD	GOOD
Color	POOR	GOOD	GOOD	POOR	POOR	POOR
Tolerance	GOOD	GOOD	FAIR	FAIR	FAIR	GOOD
Speed	GOOD	FAIR	FAIR	FAIR	FAIR	FAIR
Price (Low Volume)	FAIR	POOR	POOR	POOR	POOR	POOR
Price (High Volume)	POOR	GOOD	GOOD	GOOD	FAIR	FAIR

Figure 1-1: The various digital manufacturing process attributes.

Speeding Products to Market

One of the key advantages to digital manufacturing is the speed with which a new product can be brought to market. In traditional production, it can take weeks and months for a machine shop or other manufacturer to produce even simple parts for your product. With today's competitive marketplace, that time can mean that you can't bring a product to market fast enough and the result may be reduced market share or a totally missed opportunity.

Unlike traditional manufacturing, digital manufacturing means very fast turnaround. For example, rather than weeks to get a handful of machined parts shipped, with a competent digital manufacturing partner you may be able to cut that time to a single day. In many cases, the first product that reaches the market is the one that's successful, and products that are late to market never have a chance.

Moving from Prototype to Production

At some point your product may be ready to make the move from prototype into actual production. Depending on your needs, this move may involve simply ordering the additional components you need from your digital manufacturing partner, or it may involve moving to a more traditional manufacturing process. In addition, this move also means deciding upon the appropriate method of manufacturing, whether that be something like injection molding, machining, 3-D printing, or another type of manufacturing.

Projected product demand plays a big part in determining your decisions at this point. A product that will sell in the millions almost certainly calls for a different process than a product that will likely be limited to a few hundred pieces.

Even if your analysis suggests that your product will have a huge market, digital manufacturing can play an important part by enabling you to go into pilot production sooner. In this case, a quick-turn digital manufacturer can provide bridge tooling in a few weeks while you wait for your actual mass production tooling to be ready. This process typically takes months.

Going beyond Market Launch

Products often remain in a constant state of development throughout their life cycle. Although change can be difficult and costly using traditional manufacturing processes, it's much easier to update lower-volume products made using quick-turn digital manufacturing processes.

Consider, for example, an injection-molded plastic part. In traditional manufacturing, that part would be produced using a very expensive steel mold. A prototype and low-volume digital manufacturing company might produce the same part using aluminum tooling that costs a fraction of the price of a steel mold. Although the aluminum tooling might not be durable enough to produce millions of identical parts, for production runs in the thousands, and tens of thousands, the cost savings are immense.

For products that may have low-volume production throughout the product's life, you should consider digital manufacturing processes across multiple life cycle stages. I cover those in this section.

Growth and maturity

Product growth spurts can be unpredictable. If you're overly optimistic in scaling up production, you might end up with excess inventories that are costly to store as you wait for growth to begin again. Meeting market demand that only requires small runs as you grow means that you can better control costs. Low-volume digital manufacturing allows you to specify exactly the number of products you need as you grow your market.

When the peak of the market for your product is reached, the urge to enjoy the view for as long as possible can be captivating to the point of being dangerous. Reexamining the current state of the market, the competition, consumer interests, and of course, demand is important in identifying when to begin scaling down production.

Part of managing a product's life cycle is also identifying when development of its successor should begin. If a product truly remains in a perpetual state of development throughout its life, then it's possible that next version already has a framework to build on. The start of a new version's life cycle isn't staked to a particular stage of the existing product version, but when current market factors are acknowledged during growth and maturity, it's realistic that the production paths of the two products may intersect as one scales up and the other back down.

Decline

The descent back down from a product's peak can be equally as difficult as its ascent. The initial excitement of launching the product is usually diminished when a product begins its decline, so it becomes a matter of reaching eventual product obsolescence in a rational way. Maybe low-volume injection molding was used very early on in development and growth. Maybe it was never used and prototyping moved straight to high-volume steel tooling. Regardless, just-in-time (JIT) manufacturing is becoming more frequently incorporated into production plans.

Companies that are scaling down can have low-volume tooling re-created, or revisited, allowing customers to place JIT orders. JIT manufacturing eliminates the need to warehouse, or potentially write off, unused parts as they can be ordered in small runs as needed. Mitigating risk during product decline is an integral part of successful product life cycle planning as it has a direct impact on the product's profit and loss statement.

For any product, mapping a strong course up and down a production path, and employing the right manufacturing processes along the way, help ensure a successful endeavor.

Chapter 2

Comparing Additive and Subtractive Methods

*A*lthough digital manufacturing uses different technologies to quickly produce various components, machining and 3-D printing technologies can be pretty neatly divided into additive and subtractive methods of manufacturing. This chapter explains the differences between additive and subtractive methods, examines where each has strengths and weaknesses, and considers how the two methods complement each other.

Understanding the Fundamental Differences

Additive and subtractive methods both have appropriate uses in digital manufacturing, but some fundamental differences do exist between the two. It's important for you to understand these differences so you have a better feel for how these methods can be used.

Additive manufacturing

Additive manufacturing is a method of building parts by adding individual thin layers of material. As each layer is added, it serves as a base for additional layers of material.

3-D printing is an interchangeable umbrella term with additive manufacturing, but in reality, several processes fall under the additive manufacturing category. Although the commonly available 3-D printers typically built parts using melted plastic or a similar material, other additive manufacturing processes offer far more versatility in build quality and material choices. As an example, a method of *metal sintering* actually fuses layers of powder to create metal parts.

Subtractive manufacturing

Subtractive manufacturing is a method of machining parts by starting with a block of material and removing material from the places where it isn't needed into the finished part. The excess material can be removed by using different types of tools, but manufacturing processes like turning and milling are a pretty common sight.

To better visualize subtractive manufacturing, consider how a sculptor might start with a large block of stone. Using hammers and chisels, the sculptor chips away at the stone to create a statue. The statue is smaller than the original block of stone because the sculptor has subtracted the pieces of stone that didn't fit into the final design.

Nowadays, subtractive manufacturing often incorporates *computer numeric control* (CNC) machinery such as lathes and mills to produce precise parts. CNC machines are generally much faster and more precise than human operated machinery. CNC machines also offer a level of repeatability that would be a struggle for most human operators.

Injection molding is technically a type of additive process but is often lumped into the subtractive camp because subtractive methods are used to create the injection molds.

Looking at Strengths and Weaknesses of Each Method

No single manufacturing method (or material) can serve every purpose. Unfortunately, no one has yet figured out how to build the *Star Trek* replicator machine, so it's important to understand the inherent strengths and weaknesses in both additive and subtractive manufacturing methods.

Additive strengths

Because additive manufacturing builds parts out of thousands of extremely thin layers, it's possible to create highly complex geometries that may be impossible using other methods. For example, parts can incorporate internal channels and holes in places that would be unreachable by any modern milling machine. This means that a very complex assembly may be able to be manufactured in one piece as opposed to requiring several mating pieces.

Additive manufacturing also offers unique opportunities in creating very low-volume, custom pieces. Consider, for example, the possibilities that additive manufacturing provides for the dental and jewelry fields. Obviously, a custom-made denture isn't something that would be created in large quantities; instead it would be fitted to the individual.

 Although both additive and subtractive manufacturing methods share the capability of using a variety of materials, the properties of those materials often differ from one method to the other. You'll find that a knowledgeable digital manufacturing partner can offer advice in this area.

Additive weaknesses

Even though additive manufacturing is highly versatile, it doesn't fit the needs in every case for a couple of reasons:

- ✔ Additive manufacturing is best suited for small production quantities. As production scales up into the thousands and tens of thousands of pieces, additive manufacturing becomes too expensive to use on an ongoing basis.

It is typically not cost-effective to manufacture more than a few hundred additive parts. This price premium may decrease as technology improves in the future, but it is an important consideration for now if you need a lot of parts.

✔ Another weakness of additive manufacturing is the result of the way the parts are created. Unlike molded or machined parts, those made with additive methods tend to have a somewhat rougher appearance. It's often possible to polish or otherwise prepare the surface of parts made with additive methods, but this extra processing step does add to the production time and cost.

Subtractive strengths

Milling and turning are well-known processes in traditional manufacturing. Machined parts can be made from most any material that's available in a solid form. For example, many types of metal, wood, and plastic can provide the foundation for parts made using subtractive manufacturing methods.

Subtractive manufacturing tends to create parts with a very finished appearance that often need no further processing to be ready for use. Also, because machining starts with a solid block of material, you typically don't encounter porosity issues that can sometimes cause problems with additive processes. In addition, subtractive manufacturing can be less expensive than additive manufacturing due to material costs.

Subtractive weaknesses

Just as additive manufacturing methods have certain weaknesses, the same is true for subtractive manufacturing methods. For example, in order to machine an internal passage or a hole in a part, the area where these features need to be must be accessible to the tooling. Unfortunately, this requirement means that single parts may not be able to be as complex as might be possible with an additive manufacturing process. In some cases, this means that multiple parts would have to be designed so that they can be properly machined and then fit together during final assembly.

Machining is also limited by the capabilities of the tools used in manufacturing the parts. Depending on the manufacturer, there might be size limitations or minimal size restrictions on what can be machined.

Using the Methods as a Complement to Each Other

You aren't, of course, limited to producing your entire product using a single method and material. In fact, you'll probably find that different methods are appropriate for different parts of a product.

As I mention in Chapter 1, you may also find that you need to use different methods for quick prototypes than you use for finished products. For example, a rough finish may be acceptable on your 3-D-printed prototype, but customers may object to the crude feel that an additive process might produce on a part. Possible solutions include secondary finishing options, switching to a machined part, or even using injection molding during prototyping. Your digital manufacturing partner can offer advice on the method of manufacturing best suited to produce the parts you need.

No matter which digital manufacturing method turns out to be most appropriate for creating your product, you need to start with a good 3-D CAD model. The manufacturing company should be able to use this model to both provide design advice and to help select the proper manufacturing method.

Chapter 3

Looking at Different Manufacturing Materials

. . . .

In This Chapter

▶ Looking at thermoplastics, thermosets, and photopolymers

▶ Understanding plastics and plasticlike materials

▶ Examining hard and soft metals

▶ Selecting the proper process

. . . .

Digital manufacturing techniques encompass different processes that can use a range of materials. In order to choose the best material to produce your part, you need to understand which materials are available to which processes as well as some of the characteristics of those materials. This chapter looks at several different material categories to help you understand not only what's possible but also which materials may best suit your needs.

Differentiating Thermoplastics, Thermosets, and Photopolymers

In the 1967 movie *The Graduate,* Dustin Hoffman's character Benjamin Braddock was advised that there was a great future in plastics. Even if he didn't follow that advice, the manufacturing industry certainly has, and it uses many types of plastics and plasticlike materials.

To the uninitiated, the many different types of plastics and plasticlike materials can be confusing for a few reasons:

✔ There's a general gap in understanding the fundamental relationship between the internal structure of the material and its properties.

✔ Accurately defining application requirements is usually given insufficient time and attention.

✔ Even when these first two hurdles are overcome, finding accurate property data for materials can be hard.

Determining the appropriate material for your application involves putting together information from a variety of incomplete sources. Material data sheets are the primary source of information, and you should figure out how to extract as much information as possible from this source. More detailed information can sometimes be obtained from design manuals and application notes published by individual material suppliers and can fill in the gaps in the data sheet. Supplemental information is usually more available for higher performance engineering and specialty materials than it is for commodity materials. If you really want to understand a material, you need to be prepared to do a little detective work and some testing.

Thermoplastics

Thermoplastics are a type of plastic that becomes moldable above a certain temperature and then solidifies upon cooling. Thermoplastics are typically used in injection molding. Another term for this type of plastic is *thermosoftening*. As this term implies, thermoplastics can be resoftened by heating.

The technical term for what happens to a thermoplastic when it's heated is a *phase change*. A very common example of the material undergoing a phase change is what happens to water at freezing temperature. Below that temperature the water is solid, but above that temperature the water is liquid.

Some common thermoplastics include:

✔ Acetal, also called Delrin

✔ Acrylic

✔ Acrylonitrile butadiene styrene (ABS)

- ✔ Nylon
- ✔ Polycarbonate
- ✔ Polyethylene
- ✔ Polylactic acid (PLA)
- ✔ Polypropylene
- ✔ Polystyrene
- ✔ Polytetrafluoroethylene (PTE), also called Teflon
- ✔ Polyvinyl chloride (PVC)

Thermosets

The name *thermoset* may seem a little confusing, especially compared to thermoplastic (see the preceding section). A thermoset material is one that irreversibly cures instead of being something that can be resoftened. Probably the easiest way to remember the difference is that while a thermoplastic remains plastic, a thermoset takes a permanent set.

Thermoset materials can be cured through a chemical reaction or through irradiation, depending on the particular composition of the material. Liquid silicone rubber is a common example of a moldable thermoset material.

These thermoset materials are generally stronger than thermoplastic materials and are also used for various molding processes. A few examples of thermoset materials include:

- ✔ Bakelite
- ✔ Epoxy
- ✔ Melamine
- ✔ Polyurethanes (also found in thermoplastics, though less frequently)
- ✔ RTV
- ✔ Silicone rubber

Photopolymers

Photopolymers are plastics that change their properties when exposed to light. These plastics are typically cured using ultraviolet light, and they cure quite rapidly. Photopolymers are often used in 3-D printing (and similar processes).

Photopolymers tend to be more brittle than other types of plastics, and they often are unstable when exposed to sunlight or high humidity.

Like thermoset materials, photopolymers experience a one-way change during curing and can't be resoftened once they've cured. When used in processes like 3-D printing, photopolymers are cured layer by layer. Typically this is accomplished by using something like a UV laser to draw (and cure) a layer of the part on the resin before lowering the table deeper into the resin the width of one layer. Then the next layer is drawn and cured and the process continues until the entire part has been formed.

Various photosensitive polymer resins are used as photopolymers in the digital manufacturing process.

Comparing Plastics to Plasticlike Materials

Technically speaking, not everything that appears to be plastic is actually plastic. Thermoset and photopolymer materials behave differently than true plastics, but you'll be forgiven if you allow the experts the game of figuring out which is which. Still, it can be interesting to compare plastics and plasticlike materials.

Stereolithography (a commonly used additive manufacturing process that can be shortened to *SL*) materials are photopolymers rather than thermoplastics, and, as such, are different from common engineering-grade resins in several key properties. These plasticlike materials can still be very useful to designers, though, for form, fit, and limited functional testing if they match up to the intended production material to some extent. Typically, the most important property that designers want to emulate is stiffness (or tensile modulus, in technical terms). So, when a manufacturer offers an *ABS-like* material, its likeness to ABS is due to its similar stiffness.

The properties of SL materials that most often differ from engineering-grade thermoplastics are *elongation to break* (how much it stretches before it breaks, measured in percent) and temperature capability (how hot you can get it before it softens).

All polymers have a long-term sensitivity to oxygen, and this sensitivity increases at higher temperatures. Degradation associated with aging is captured by a property called the *relative thermal index* (RTI). This value comes from a test mandated and administered by Underwriters Laboratories. It is currently the best gauge for measuring the long-term effects of aging on the mechanical and electrical properties of polymers. RTI testing begins by measuring key baseline properties. Test specimens are then aged at multiple temperatures and the baseline properties are monitored until they decline to 50 percent of the original values. The time required to reach 50 percent performance is called the *time to failure*.

Examining Hard and Soft Metals

Of course, not all parts are best made from plastics. Often, metal is the more appropriate choice. You can choose either hard or soft metals depending on what's best for a particular part.

Soft metals: Aluminum, magnesium, brass, and copper

Aluminum is the most abundant metal on the planet and the third most common element after oxygen and silicon. In fact, you might be surprised to learn that aluminum makes up 8 percent of the total mass of the earth's crust!

Aluminum is soft and highly malleable, so by itself it's a poor candidate for mechanical purposes. Aluminum is usually blended with other elements, including silicon, copper, magnesium, and zinc, then heat-treated to make the strong, lightweight alloys used today in airframes, automobiles, and various consumer products.

Another popular lightweight material is magnesium. Two-thirds the weight of typical aluminum alloys and nearly as strong, it is the lightest of all structural metals. Magnesium is a preferred material wherever good strength and low weight is important. It has excellent dampening characteristics, is easily machined, and readily molded or die-cast.

Two other soft metals are brass and copper. Of the two, brass is by far the most versatile. With the exception of environments high in ammonia and some acids, it is extremely weather and corrosion resistant. If you've ever replaced a car radiator, soldered a kitchen faucet, or played the French horn, you've handled parts made of brass.

Hard metals: Steel, stainless steel, titanium, cobalt chrome, and Inconel

Some parts need to be made from hard metals. Steel is mostly composed of iron, the next most abundant element after aluminum. Iron smelting and limited steel manufacturing has been in use for thousands of years, but it wasn't until the mid-1800s that mass production of high-quality steel was made possible.

As with soft metals, a small quantity of alloying elements can have a dramatic effect on steel's properties — the addition of less than 1 percent carbon and manganese is what makes brittle iron into tough 1018 steel. And 4140 alloy steel, suitable for aircraft use, is made by combining an equally small amount of chromium along with a dusting of molybdenum.

Carbon steels such as these can be hardened to one extent or another, and are easily welded. There's just one problem: They rust, making plating or painting a requirement for most any application involving carbon steel.

To combat rust you can use stainless steel. By increasing the amount of chromium to at least 10.5 percent, corrosion resistance is greatly enhanced. Stainless steel is widely used in the chemical industry, textile processing, and for marine applications. Many stainless steels are temperature resistant as well, and are able to withstand temperatures upwards of 2700 degrees F, hot enough to turn aluminum, brass, and copper into molten puddles.

The 300-series stainless steels carry at least 20 percent chromium along with a fair amount of nickel, making them very difficult to machine.

17-4 PH stainless steel is a versatile but very tough material that contains nickel, chromium, and copper. Although considered part of the stainless steel family, its machinability in the annealed state approaches super alloy status — when heat treated, it easily achieves hardness of 45 Rc and tensile strength of 150,000 psi or higher, three times that of carbon steel. It's most commonly used where a combination of high strength and good corrosion resistance is needed.

Then, there's titanium. This lightweight element is often alloyed with aluminum and vanadium, providing a strong, corrosion-resistant material. Like cobalt chrome, titanium is biocompatible, and is used extensively for bone screws, pins, and plates. This makes titanium appealing to the aerospace industry and high-performance vehicle manufacturers.

In the category of truly robust alloys, you might consider cobalt chrome or Inconel. Inconel contains 50 percent or more of nickel, giving it excellent strength at a range of temperatures. It's used for extreme demands such as gas turbine blades, jet engine compressor discs, and even nuclear reactors and jet engine combustion chambers. Sitting right next to nickel on the periodic table is cobalt, the main ingredient in cobalt chrome alloy.

Unfortunately, cobalt chrome and Inconel are generally considered too difficult to machine, so they're more often used in additive manufacturing using the direct metal laser sintering (DMLS) process.

Choosing the Right Process

Sometimes, the same material can be used in more than one digital manufacturing process. For example, some plastic materials like nylon are suitable for both 3-D printing and injection molding. Likewise, certain metals such as aluminum and stainless steel can be used in 3-D printing, machining, and molding processes.

Choosing the right process for plastics and metals used in multiple technologies involves three factors:

- ✔ The use to which the part will be placed
- ✔ The complexity of the part design
- ✔ The volume of the production run

Check out Chapters 4, 5, and 6 for more information on the major digital manufacturing processes.

Choosing a plastic

It's really not possible to make a full material recommendation without understanding the complete application requirements for the part. Sometimes, though, it's not cost-effective to fully engineer the part to come up with a material selection. Here are a few quick rules of thumb:

- ✔ Try ABS. ABS works for many, many applications. It's reasonably priced, strong, relatively tough, has a decent appearance, and is forgiving even if you don't follow all the standard design rules for plastic parts. It does have a relatively low melting point.

- ✔ If it needs to be cheap and rigidity and cosmetics aren't really important, try polypropylene (PP).

- ✔ If you need something a little tougher than ABS or able to withstand a little higher temperature, try polycarbonate (PC). PC

is less forgiving than ABS if you don't follow the standard design rules for plastic parts.

- ✔ If it needs to be nice-looking and transparent, try acrylic (PMMA). PMMA can be a little brittle. A transparent PC will be tougher than PMMA but a little less cosmetically nice.

- ✔ If these rules don't point you where you need to go, then you need to start doing the math and analysis.

If you're going to use injection-molded parts, you might try machining a couple test parts in the target material before committing to a mold. Molds are designed to match the rate at which a particular resin shrinks as it solidifies, so it may not be possible to run multiple resins in the same mold without risk to part size, tolerances, and/or dimensions.

Chapter 4

Exploring 3-D Printing

3-D printing is an umbrella term that's often used to loosely describe all additive manufacturing processes. These days, most people probably associate the term with a device somewhat akin to an inkjet printer, but that narrow view doesn't come close to understanding the many versatile options available today. This chapter provides a brief introduction to 3-D printing, looks at important processes that fall under this umbrella, discusses some design considerations you need to be aware of, and considers what comes next.

Understanding 3-D Printing

Different additive manufacturing processes fulfill different design needs. Although these processes vary considerably, you want to understand their shared characteristics before moving onto the specifics of each process.

The process

The additive manufacturing process builds parts by building very thin layers of material. There are several methods of joining layers of material into solid objects, including extruding, jetting, fusing, or curing. Regardless of the specific method that's used in a process, each layer of material is laid down individually and then the material is bonded to the layers below to form the part.

The equipment

When it comes to digital manufacturing, having high-quality equipment really matters. While a simple desktop 3-D printer might be sufficient for a weekend tinkerer to knock out a crude toy soldier or rudimentary prototype, the equipment needed to produce high-grade prototypes or parts for commercial projects is much more complex, capable, and expensive.

The equipment used for additive manufacturing varies according to the process that's used, but basically it needs to be able to place the material with extreme precision. Depending on the process, there may also be a requirement to fuse or bond the material in place (some processes use materials that automatically bond to the existing material layers).

In addition to using reliable additive equipment and materials, manufacturing high-quality prototypes depends on elevated levels of very sophisticated computing power to build precision parts. A digital manufacturing company often merges these three benefits.

The purpose

Building a part in thousands of thin layers provides the opportunity to create highly complex geometries that may be impossible to machine or mold. Additive manufacturing is especially attractive for rapidly creating prototypes, but in some cases it's also appropriate for small quantities of production parts. Quite simply, developing parts without the need for additional design planning that usually goes into injection molding or CNC machining makes it possible to quickly explore your design options without some of the limitations you might encounter in more traditional manufacturing processes.

Looking at the Major Processes

In this section, I give you the various 3-D printing processes, which helps you better understand whether a certain process can fit your needs during different stages of prototyping and part production.

Binder jetting

Binder jetting (BJET) is one of the simplest and most basic additive prototyping processes. An inkjet print head moves across a bed of powder, selectively depositing a liquid binding material. A new layer of unbound powder is placed over the partially bound layer, and the process is repeated until the complete part has been formed. After completion, the unbound powder is removed, leaving the finished object.

Binder jetting offers the following advantages:

- ✔ Fast production
- ✔ Low cost
- ✔ Easily produced in various colors
- ✔ Ease of duplication of complex geometries

Binder jetting also has some disadvantages:

- ✔ Rough surface
- ✔ Low part strength
- ✔ Not suitable for functional testing

Stereolithography

Stereolithography (SL) uses a computer controlled ultraviolet laser to cure parts in a pool of photopolymer resin. As each layer is drawn by the laser, the part is lowered in the pool of liquid resin, allowing the next layer of liquid to be solidified. The quality of the finished part depends largely on the quality of the equipment used in the SL process, shown in Figure 4-1.

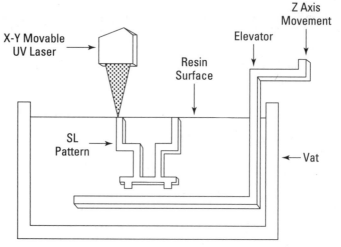

Figure 4-1: The SL process.

There are three main advantages to using the SL process:

- ✔ Moderate price
- ✔ Ease of duplication of complex geometries
- ✔ One of the best surface finishes for an additive process

The SL process also has certain disadvantages that include low part strength, cured resin becoming brittle over time, and parts having limited use for functional testing.

Fused deposition modeling

Fused deposition modeling (FDM) melts and resolidifies thermoplastic resin (often ABS, polycarbonate, or ABS/polycarbonate blend) in layers to form a finished prototype. Because it uses real thermoplastic resins, parts are stronger than those produced by some processes, and may be of some limited use for functional testing.

Some advantages of the FDM process include the following:

- ✔ Moderate price
- ✔ Moderate strength
- ✔ A partial match to the physical characteristics of ABS or polycarbonate parts
- ✔ Ease of duplication of complex geometries

FDM also has some disadvantages:

- ✔ Rippled surface on parts
- ✔ Parts that are very porous
- ✔ Limited suitability for functional testing
- ✔ Slow production; can take days to produce large parts
- ✔ Poor strength on the z-axis

PolyJet

PolyJet (PJET) uses a print head to spray layers of photopolymer resin that are cured, one after another, using ultraviolet light. The layers are very thin, allowing superior resolution. The material is supported by a gel matrix that is removed after completion of the part.

Some advantages of the PJET process include good surface finish and ease of duplication of complex geometries. But the disadvantages include things such as limited resin choice, poor strength, and costly materials.

Selective laser sintering

Selective laser sintering (SLS) employs a computer controlled CO_2 (carbon dioxide) laser to fuse layers of powdered plastic material such as nylon from the bottom up. Strength is better than that of SL but lower than that produced by processes like injection molding or CNC machining. SLS has some use as a production method.

SLS offers several advantages:

✔ Moderate price

✔ Offers very good accuracy

✔ More durable than some other processes, such as SL

✔ Suitable for some functional testing

✔ Ease of duplication of complex geometries

The disadvantages of SLS include the fact that you have a limited choice of resin and the surface finish is often rough.

Digital light processing

Digital light processing (DLP)-based additive manufacturing digitally slices a solid into layers, which a Texas Instruments DLP chip projects, one after another, onto the surface of a liquid photopolymer bath. The projected light hardens a layer of liquid polymer resting on a movable build plate. The build plate moves down in small increments as new images are projected onto the liquid, hardening each subsequent layer to produce the finished object. The remaining liquid polymer is then drained from the vat, leaving the solid model. The process can be useful for producing a limited number of small, highly detailed parts but is less suitable for larger parts, especially those requiring smooth finishes.

The advantages of DLP include the following:

✔ It's a relatively fast process.

✔ Parts are competitively priced.

✔ High resolution is possible.

✔ It can produce very complex shapes.

Some disadvantages of DLP are:

✔ Limited choice of resins

✔ May not be suitable for functional testing

✔ Surfaces that may be rough

Direct metal laser sintering

Direct metal laser sintering (DMLS) is the leading additive method for making metal prototypes. It's similar to selective laser sintering of plastic resin but instead uses metals, including aluminum, stainless steel, titanium, cobalt chrome, and Inconel. It offers good accuracy and detail and excellent mechanical properties. DMLS can be used for very small parts and features, and because it's an additive process, it can reproduce geometries that may be impossible to machine, such as partially enclosed spaces.

Secondary operations are almost always required on parts produced by DMLS and can include drilling, slotting, milling, and reaming, and finishing procedures, including anodizing, electro-polishing, hand polishing, and powder coating or painting.

DMLS offers some important advantages:

- ✔ Can use nearly any metal alloy
- ✔ Mechanical properties essentially equal to those of conventionally formed parts
- ✔ Can use geometries that are impossible to machine or cast

DMLS also has some disadvantages:

- ✔ It is a relatively slow process.
- ✔ Parts can be expensive.
- ✔ It requires considerable expertise to make quality parts.
- ✔ Parts usually require expensive post processing.

Allowing for Design Considerations

A few important design considerations affect how your part can be made. For example, the type of process used has a direct effect on things like the resolution that can be obtained.

In some cases, this may be a limiting factor in terms of how fine part details may be.

In some cases, it may be necessary to modify your design to include internal supports. The need for supports depends on factors such as the physical design and the material composition of the part. Your digital manufacturing partner should be able to provide advice about supports, if the process you choose requires that.

You may also encounter cost considerations relating to things such as the material selected and the physical volume of the part. Depending on the process that's used, suitable plastic materials include:

- ✔ ABS
- ✔ Nylon
- ✔ Polycarbonate
- ✔ Polyether ether ketone (PEEK)
- ✔ Polyetherimide (PEI)
- ✔ Polypropylene

Suitable metals include:

- ✔ Aluminum
- ✔ Cobalt chrome
- ✔ Inconel
- ✔ Stainless steel
- ✔ Titanium

Chapter 3 discusses materials in more detail, but Table 4-1 provides a brief recap of the materials that are adaptable to some of the processes.

You'll want to consider factors such as part strength and finish when choosing both the appropriate process and material.

Table 4-1	Additive Process Comparison		
Process	**Strength in psi**	**Finish (typ.)**	**Materials**
SL, DLP	2,500-10,000	0.002-0.006 in. 0.051-0.152 mm	Thermoplastic-like photopolymers
FDM	5,200-9,800	0.005-0.013 in. 0.127-0.330 mm	ABS, PC, PC/ABS, PPSU, PEI
PJET	7,200-8,750	0.0006-0.0012 in. 0.015-0.030 mm	Acrylic-based photopolymers, elastomeric photopolymers
SLS	5,300-11,300	0.004 in. 0.102 mm	Nylon, metals
DMLS	37,700-190,000	0.0008-0.0012 in. 0.020-0.030 mm	Stainless steel, titanium, chrome, aluminums, Inconel

Finishing Up after 3-D Printing

Both the intended use and the process selected can be important factors in determining the suitability of a part at the point it comes away from the manufacturing process. For example, a part that's simply a concept model designed to give an idea of the size and shape of a finished product needs no further processing. At the opposite end of the spectrum might be an end-use metal component built by DMLS that's used in an aircraft, for example. In that case, the part may need additional processing such as anodizing to protect it or a heat treatment to strengthen it.

Chapter 5

Using the Subtractive Process with CNC Machining

● ●

In This Chapter

▶ Introducing CNC machining

▶ Getting to know machining processes

▶ Looking at design considerations for machining

▶ Finishing your parts

● ●

*C*omputer numeric control (CNC) machining is a subtractive process used in digital manufacturing. Rather than building parts up layer-by-layer as is the case in additive processes, CNC machining starts with a solid piece of material and removes what isn't needed.

This chapter provides a brief introduction to CNC machining, looks at the processes that fall under this category, discusses some design considerations you need to be aware of, and considers what you may need to do when your part is completed.

Understanding CNC Machining

CNC machining uses computer programming to control the operation of machine tools. These tools remove excess material from the original block or billet to produce the desired part.

Although CNC machining is often used in traditional manufacturing, the digital manufacturing industry has turned the existing model on its head. In the past, the nonrecurring engineering (NRE) costs involved in programming CNC machines, as well as building fixtures to support the machining process, meant that CNC machining had a long payback requiring large volume production in order to be economically reasonable. Digital manufacturing companies have figured out ways to automate both the programming and fixturing for many types of parts. The result of this automation is that in many cases digital manufacturers can produce small quantities of CNC machined parts at far more reasonable prices than were possible in the past.

The process

The CNC machining process begins with a set of computer instructions that direct the operation of the machinery. In digital manufacturing, these instructions are generated by powerful computers that analyze the 3-D CAD model you've created of your part. The specialized computers that perform this analysis also look for problems that might result in issues preventing the part from being properly formed. For example, designs are analyzed to make sure that they don't include undercuts that are impossible to machine. Of course, the analysis also considers a range of other problems, too. Depending on the geometry of the part that's desired, the piece of material may be fixed in place for machining or it may be rotated against the tooling.

The equipment

The actual equipment used in CNC machining varies according to the part that's being produced, but in each case, the tooling and the part move relative to each other. In the case of a lathe, it's the part that rotates against the tooling. With milling machines, the part is generally fixed in place and the tooling moves. In some cases, both types of operations may be needed in order to fully machine the part. For example, a lathe may be used to produce a cylindrical part that then needs a cross-drilled, threaded hole after the part has been turned.

Fixturing is an important part of the CNC machining process. It makes sure that the part is always in the proper physical relationship relative to the tooling.

Fixturing can be expensive to produce, so you'll want to verify the cost upfront. Some digital manufacturing companies like Proto Labs don't separately charge for fixturing, which can result in large savings on your parts.

The purpose

CNC machining can serve a few purposes. In addition to creating prototype parts for form, fit, and function, this process can also be very useful for rapidly creating production parts, jigs and fixtures, and one-offs.

Looking at Major Machining Processes

CNC machining isn't a single process; instead several different types of machining may be used depending on the parts being produced. In each case, though, the machines are computer-controlled so they produce precisely the part that's called for in your design.

It was once a no-brainer. Round parts were turned on lathes; non-round parts were machined on mills. With the advent of CNC machining centers, which interpolate round part features with ease, the line between the two machining processes became blurred. The situation grew even more confusing when CNC lathes attained live-tool capability. Operations that were once the exclusive domain of the milling department were now coming off the lathe complete. As a result, deciding which machine is the best fit for producing any given part has become more complicated than it once was.

Some parts are obvious lathe candidates. Consider the piston for a gas engine. The long length to diameter ratios of the component, coupled with complex external geometry and challenging internal features, makes it a permanent resident of the turning department. Conversely, the engine block that mates with the piston — with its large milled surfaces, detailed pockets, and intersecting bores — will never be spun on a lathe, no matter how live-tool capable that machine may be.

Three-axis milling

The first type of CNC machining process to consider is *three-axis milling*. A three-axis milling machine moves the tool along an X, Y, and Z axis. This makes it fairly easy to visualize as you get accustomed to 3-D being described in terms of X, Y, and Z.

Moving the tool in combinations of two or more axes at the same time makes it possible to create complex shapes and cuts. The tool is held perpendicular to a table where the work piece is held with a clamp or fixture.

To perform different operations, the operator or the machine itself can switch the tools that are used to perform different activities using the right tool for the job. In addition to milling, these machines can perform drilling and tapping operations, as long as the axis of the hole is in line with the Z axis of the machine, and the hole isn't obstructed by an overhang.

Five-axis milling

Another machining option is five-axis milling. Whereas three-axis milling moves the tool in X, Y, and Z dimensions, five-axis milling adds two more axes to the operation.

With these machines, the tool, work piece, or both can be rotated around additional axes while it's moving along any or all of the other three axes. This allows the tool or the work piece to be held in position or moved in ways that accommodate more complex geometry than a three-axis machine could achieve.

Parts with extreme geometry like turbine blades, compound or overhung surfaces, or with complex internal geometry are all prime candidates for five-axis milling. The necessity to have the spinning tool duck under overhangs or to place hole features in any direction necessitates adding stronger capabilities than a three-axis operation would allow or adding additional discrete operations to augment the work that the three-axis machine performed.

Turning

Traditionally, a machine called a *lathe* was used to turn round parts. The part was fastened between the headstock and the tailstock on the lathe and then rotated against fixed tooling. The digital manufacturing industry has greatly redefined the turning process. Now, turning is still used to create round parts, especially those with a long length to diameter ratios. But some newer machines combine the capabilities of a lathe with live-tool equipped three-axis milling.

If you're still unsure about what parts are lathe-worthy, consider a few household objects. A pint glass, for example, with its smooth, regular shape and length several times greater than the outside diameter, is a straightforward exercise on a lathe. Not so on a machining center. A coffee cup, on the other hand, with its jutting handle and finger-ready hole, is impossible to turn. Here, only a mill will do.

Those 3-lb. dumbbells collecting dust in the closet could be turned fairly easily on a lathe. The wide, relatively deep recessed area where your hand grips the bar can be turned with a simple grooving routine, a feature that would be difficult to cut on a mill.

A tea cup saucer could go either way. Interpolating the concentric ridges and curved surfaces is equally possible on a mill or a lathe. That said, it would almost certainly be faster to turn the saucer, and far more efficient in terms of material use.

You may find that turned surfaces are smoother and more round than their milled counterparts. Milled features may have visible tool marks, which you can bead blast to give the surfaces a matte finish and knock down any small burrs that remain after the machining process.

Examining Design Considerations for Digital Manufacturing

CNC machining offers a reliable digital manufacturing solution, but like all manufacturing processes, there are design considerations to keep in mind. Being aware of these considerations will allow you to plan for the best possible parts.

Don't overlook the details. It's easy to focus on the primary shapes and features of a part when thinking about how it could be made using digital manufacturing processes. There are details that have to be considered as well when you're looking at using CNC machining for a digital manufacturing process.

Threaded holes

Threaded holes are often used to allow objects to be attached to parts. These types of holes normally require a secondary operation and sometimes require that part be removed from the fixture and set up in a different way. Because of this, a large number of holes may limit a quick turnaround or require the use of a different manufacturing process.

Newer lathes used by digital manufacturing companies often have milling capability. Drilling a side hole or milling a flat is well within their means, as long as that feature is parallel or perpendicular to the long axis of the part. If a hole can be drilled, threading the hole as necessary is probably also within the capacity of the machinery.

Text on parts

It's not uncommon to add a company's name, logo, or part number on individual parts. Depending on your needs, these can appear as raised characters or they may be engraved into the surface of the part. Adding text, logos, or special characters to parts may either require a change in fixture or a change in tooling that requires a significant slowdown in processing speed. Most importantly, there are limits on the width, depth, and detail that can be created in a reasonable amount of time. Small text is often problematic in digital manufacturing. Check out Figure 5-1 for an example of working text into a mold.

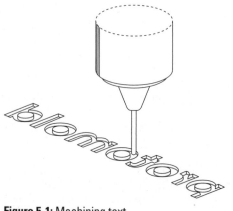

Figure 5-1: Machining text.

Materials

A range of materials are suitable for digital manufacturing. Typically, this selection covers the gamut from various types of plastics to metals. When dealing with metals, they're usually classified as either hard or soft, depending on the precise metal or alloy that's selected. Steel, stainless steel, and super alloys are on one side of the fence, and brass, copper, magnesium, and aluminum on the other.

Hard metals used in digital manufacturing include:

- ✔ Stainless steel
- ✔ Steel
- ✔ Titanium

Soft metal choices include:

- ✔ Aluminum
- ✔ Brass
- ✔ Copper
- ✔ Magnesium

Plastics used include:

- ✔ Acetal
- ✔ Acrylic
- ✔ Acrylonitrile butadiene styrene (ABS)
- ✔ Nylon
- ✔ Polycarbonate
- ✔ Polypropylene
- ✔ Polyvinyl chloride (PVC)
- ✔ Polyether ether ketone (PEEK)
- ✔ Polyetherimide (PEI)

Finishing Up after Machining

Secondary operations are common in manufacturing, especially with metal parts. Heat-treating improves strength and removes internal stresses created during raw material processing and with heavy machining. Carbon steels such as 1018 can be case hardened through nitriding or carburization, and 4140 is easily brought to 50 Rc or harder through quench and temper methods. 17-4 PH can be made quite hard, as can some 400-series stainless steels, but 300-series stainless can only be hardened through cold working or drawing through a die. Soft metals such as aluminum and magnesium are never hardened, although they may be cryogenically stress-relieved or aged by gentle heating at cookie-baking temperatures.

Plating is another common post-machining process. Aluminum is often anodized, giving it a scratch resistant surface in most any color under the sun. For non-decorative protection, chemical film or chromate is a good option. These methods also work on magnesium, although different chemicals are needed. Copper and brass discolor when exposed to oxygen, so electroless nickel or chrome plating may be applied if protection is needed. Stainless steel and super alloys require no such protection, but steel is commonly given black oxide surface treatment, or plated with nickel, cadmium, zinc, and other materials. Painting is also a popular choice, but bead blasting or some other form of abrasive preparation is recommended in order to provide a clean, rust-free surface prior to paint application.

Machined plastic parts may also need some post-production processing, but the available options are more limited than with metal parts.

Bead blasting, as the name implies, uses a high-pressure stream of particles such as glass beads to smooth sharp edges and remove burrs. Tumbling uses small ceramic or plastic media in a vibratory bowl to achieve the same effect. These processes may add a few hours to a week or more to product delivery times, depending on order quantity and part configuration. In most cases, customers can have their parts plated, painted, or anodized immediately afterwards.

Many of the same post-production processes can also be applied to parts produced using the additive manufacturing techniques discussed in Chapter 4.

Chapter 6

Producing Injection-Molded Parts

*M*ost plastic parts are created in a process called *injection molding,* which involves injecting molten plastic into a cavity in a device called a mold. However, it's not only plastic parts that can be made using injection molding. In fact, many injection-molded parts are made from liquid silicone rubber or metal. Knowing how injection molding works makes it easier to design parts for the process. This chapter gives you an understanding of the injection molding process.

Introducing Injection Molding

Injection molding is a simple process to describe, but as with most types of manufacturing, looks can be deceiving. There's actually a lot of science behind the process because you need to be aware of factors such as how the material will flow into the mold, how the size and shape will change as the material solidifies in the mold, and design guidelines that help improve the moldability of a part.

The injection molding process

The injection molding process can be broken down into a few basic steps:

1. **Melt (liquefy) the material.**

2. **Inject the molten material into the mold.**

3. **Let the molded part cool.**

4. **Eject the part from the mold.**

5. **Depending on the material used, do additional processing to create a finished part (see "Metal injection molding" later in this chapter).**

The equipment used for injection molding

Although differences do exist in the equipment used for different injection molding processes, the presses are similar regardless of the process. Within the press, you have a reservoir of the material, a means of heating the material into a state where it can flow, a high-pressure system to inject the material into the mold, and the mold itself.

In injection molding, the terms *mold* and *tool* are often used interchangeably because the mold ultimately forms the shape of the finished product. One of the differences between traditional injection molding and the way that injection molding is often done in quick-turn digital manufacturing is the type of material used for the mold. Traditionally, molds are made of steel, are designed for high volume production, and are expensive to produce. Digital manufacturing companies like Proto Labs usually machine molds from aluminum rather than steel. This change means that molds typically are designed for lower volume production, can sometimes be modified to adjust for minor design changes, and are less expensive to produce. In addition, these digital manufacturers are able to make molds far more quickly, which drastically cuts the time it takes to produce custom injection-molded parts.

The purpose of injection molding

Injection molding is a means of producing an increased volume of identical parts versus other manufacturing processes such as 3-D printing or milling that are used for smaller quantities. In most cases (but not always), prototypes are produced first using one of those other processes, and injection molding enables the vetted part to be produced more economically and at larger scale.

Getting to Know the Major Injection Molding Processes

Injection molding actually encompasses several different processes that are designed to accommodate different types of material.

Thermoplastic injection molding

A staple of manufacturing, thermoplastic injection molding offers incredible material selection. Parts made with this process are so common that it's impossible to not encounter them in day-to-day life.

The resin pellets (and sometimes a colorant or other additives) are added to a hopper and fed into the barrel where they're melted for injection into the mold. After this mixture is completely molten and the additives are blended with the resin, a valve is opened, and the plastic is injected into the cavity of the mold. Multiple parts can be made at once in a single mold using runners to connect multiple cavities (called *multicavity molds* if all the parts in a mold are identical and *family molds* if the parts are different).

For more information on thermoplastic injection molding, you may want to have a look at *Injection Molding Part Design For Dummies* (John Wiley & Sons, Inc.).

Liquid silicone rubber molding

Liquid silicone rubber (LSR) parts are molded by mixing a chilled silicone-based resin with a catalyst and injecting the mixture into a heated mold. The heat in the mold accelerates the chemical reaction that solidifies the part. Before setting up, the material has very low viscosity, similar to water. After setting up, the material has a "rubberiness" (or *durometer*) typically ranging from about 20 to 80 on the Shore A scale.

LSR can withstand constant temperatures of up to 600°F (316°C) and intermittent temperatures of 700°F (371°C). To those more familiar with ordinary thermoplastics, it may seem counterintuitive that such a rubbery material can be used in high temperature applications, but LSR is actually made to take the heat. Unlike thermoplastics, which soften when heated, thermosets like LSR are created in high heat and, in their various forms, can easily withstand temperatures that would melt thermoplastics. This suits them well for a variety of high-heat automotive and industrial applications and for medical products that are sterilized with high heat.

In addition to high heat, LSR can typically handle low temperatures, well into double digits below 0°F, while maintaining its flexibility. The exact degree of flexibility varies with the compound, but can be very high. Different types of LSR are available in a broad range of colors as well as in grades appropriate for optical and medical applications.

LSR has excellent thermal, electrical, and chemical resistance properties, but it can be degraded by certain solvents such as gasoline or mineral spirits. There are, however, specialized LSR materials like flourosilicones that are resistant to fuels.

LSR is also approved for medical applications where it will be in contact with skin. Its stability prevents it from affecting skin or, in turn, being affected by skin contact. Some grades of LSR, when combined with the appropriate manufacturing environment, can be used in implantable applications. Its hydrophobic (water-repellent) properties make it ideal for water-handling applications. And the fact that it's fire-retardant and doesn't emit toxins or halogens when burned suits it well for a variety of safety applications.

Parts molded of LSR continue to shrink after being removed from the mold as they cool. Because of the material's flexibility, different parts of a finished piece may stick to each mold half, leaving the part hanging after the mold opens. Thus, LSR parts are typically manually removed from molds.

Metal injection molding

Metal injection molding (MIM) is a manufacturing process that can produce intricate geometries in metal parts in larger quantities. MIM parts have good strength, excellent surface finishes with mechanical properties similar to wrought materials, and can have complex shapes.

A variety of metal powders are used for MIM. Stainless steel, the most common material, is used in just under half of all MIM applications. Stainless steel 316L is frequently used because of its combined strength and corrosion resistance. 17-4 PH stainless steel is a very tough material containing nickel, chromium, and copper that is used where a combination of high strength and good corrosion resistance is needed. Low-alloy steels are the second most prevalent group used in MIM, rounded out by iron-nickel alloys and specialty metals such as titanium and tungsten. Although aluminum feedstock is available, its use in MIM is rare. Because aluminum is a soft metal, other metalworking processes such as machining or casting tend to be more common. For hard metals such as stainless or low-alloy carbon steels, machining and casting become more problematic, and MIM may work better.

 Metal injection-molded parts require relatively large gates compared to plastic injection-molded parts, due to the high metal content of the feedstock. Molds for MIM parts are typically polished to some degree to help prevent the parts from sticking in the mold during ejection.

MIM requires additional steps after molding called debinding and sintering, which require upfront design considerations. The part comes out of the mold as a *green* part, meaning that it is quite fragile and still contains a binding agent. Green parts need to be processed to remove most of the binder creating a *brown* part. The brown part must then be heated (sintered) in a furnace to remove the remaining binder and to form a fully dense metal part.

A MIM part shrinks by about 20 percent during sintering, which means MIM molds need to be oversized to account for this. Also, the MIM part responds to gravity during the sintering process. Most of the polymer binder is removed during sintering, leaving just enough binder to hold the very fine metal particles clinging together for the sintering furnace. During the sintering stage, the part becomes soft as the metal powders partially melt and join together. As a part shrinks, some of it slides on the supporting surface to reach the final position. An ideal radially symmetric part would shrink uniformly to the center, so the outside edges would move the most, the center would not move at all, and the center of mass would stay in the same spot during the process. Parts need to be designed for proper support during the sintering process to ensure that they maintain their desired shape. The easiest parts to sinter have a common co-planar surface that can rest flat on a ceramic substrate or setter. When unsupported features are present, support often needs to be added through special fixturing to minimize or eliminate distortion of the part.

Die casting

Die casting is a manufacturing process that produces geometrically complex metallic parts by injecting molten aluminum or zinc at a high pressure into reusable molds (called dies) made of high-quality tool steel. Aluminum ingots, for example, are melted and maintained in a molten state in a furnace before being ladled into a shot sleeve and forced under high pressure into a mold to make a casting. High-pressure die casting machines generate high injection pressures while holding the mold halves together to resist the pressure of the injected material, enabling the production of dense parts.

Unlike metal injection molding, die casting does not use another material for binding. It is just molten material such as zinc or aluminum introduced into the cavity under pressure. The resulting parts aren't quite as strong as those created by CNC machining blocks of the same materials, but they still have many uses and can have additional processes applied to them.

Magnesium thixomolding

Magnesium thixomolding is a process of molding fully dense magnesium parts, similar to those produced in die casting, using an injection molding press. In the thixomolding process, chipped magnesium feedstock is heated in the barrel of the press. A reciprocating screw works the material into a *thixotropic* state and the material is forced into a steel mold at high speed and pressure, creating the part. In the thixotropic state, the material viscosity decreases when subjected to shear forces caused by the injection process. The low-viscosity material can fill more intricate molds with thinner walls than can be used in a die-casting process. Magnesium thixomolding produces strong, lightweight magnesium parts that maintain detailed features and can have thin walls.

Unlike quick-turn plastic injection molding aluminum tooling, a thixomolding tool is fabricated from tool steel using a combination of CNC milling and CNC electrical-discharge machining (EDM).

Gate and vent design are very important to the proper formation of the part. The part must fill smoothly and without excess turbulence, and quite a bit of the leading edge of the material is pushed all the way through the part and out into the vent system. Parts rapidly fill the mold and quickly become solid. After solidification, the parts are ejected from the press and the cycle repeats.

After ejection, parts are loaded individually into a de-gating system. For rapid thixomolding, this de-gating system consists of one or more fixtures designed to hold the part in a CNC-milling machine. The de-gating system removes the vestiges of the gate and vents, and applies any required secondary machining operations that couldn't be formed as part of the molding process (for example, internal threads).

Magnesium is often used to reduce the weight of parts in automotive and aerospace applications.

Looking at Insert Molding and Overmolding

Sometimes, injection-molded parts can be augmented using processes known as overmolding and insert molding. Essentially, these processes modify parts to make them more useful.

Overmolding

Overmolding is a process where an injection-molded part is placed into a second mold and then has another material added to it. If you've ever used a toothbrush that has a rubberized grip molded onto the plastic handle, you've encountered an overmolded part. In a high-volume application, overmolding can be done using a special press (a two-shot press) that is capable of switching one half of the mold and injecting both types of material.

Overmolding is used in many applications (often for hand-held objects), including medical devices, parts with soft grip handles such as paintbrushes, and various types of knobs. Depending on what's needed, overmolding can be done with either hard or soft plastics. Typically, a soft material is used to provide things like an improved feeling grip while a hard material may be used to strengthen or protect the part. Overmolding is also used to create an integral seal on one part that will be used in an assembly of other plastics parts.

Because overmolding eliminates a bonding step that would otherwise be needed to fasten individual parts together, this process often reduces the overall cost of manufacturing the part. In addition, overmolded parts are usually stronger than compound parts made by bonding a couple of pieces with adhesive. Overmolding also ensures proper alignment of the second material.

Insert molding

Rather than adding another element to the outside of a molded piece, *insert molding* adds something into the molded piece. A prime example of an insert molded piece may be a plastic knob that has a metal insert that fits on a shaft. Another example would be a threaded metal insert allowing a part to be bolted to a mount.

In addition to often being stronger than other types of parts, insert molded parts can be less expensive to produce because there is no need for adhesives or other fasteners.

Understanding Molding Design Considerations

Injection molding has its own special design considerations that you need to be aware of. I cover those in this section.

Draft

Injection-molded parts need to be removed from the mold after the molding process is completed. But ejecting the part can be difficult without the proper design. For example, a part with deep, straight walls tends to want to stick in the mold rather than easily popping out. This is why ice cubes aren't true cubes — if they were, they wouldn't want to come out of the ice cube tray.

One solution to making it easier to eject molded parts is to design them so that they have *draft* (a taper) on the sides. Draft facilitates the removal of the part from the mold and is particularly important in injection molding where it is most practical to eject the part using ejector pins. Figure 6-1 illustrates draft in injection molding.

Drafted

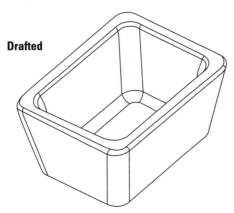

Figure 6-1: An example of draft in injection molding.

The draft angle needed to make parts eject easily from the mold varies according to the material used, the surface texture of the mold, and the depth of the part. For example, smoother parts require less of an angle than those with a heavy texture on them.

Wall thickness

As parts made with most of the injection molding processes are more or less hollow, walls have to be made to produce exterior faces and interior faces that act as supports. Certain limits exist on how thin these walls can be, based on the material and the height of the wall. If a wall is too thin, it may not properly fill before the material starts to solidify. This can cause gaps and even prevent portions of the mold from filling at all. If the walls are too thick, they can distort the shape of the part or faces that have critical locations.

So if you need to change the thickness of the walls, make sure that the transitions are smooth to limit the stresses on the walls and minimize the differences in shrinkage as the material cools. See Figure 6-2. Sharp corners also cause stress risers in the part, becoming a potential failure point.

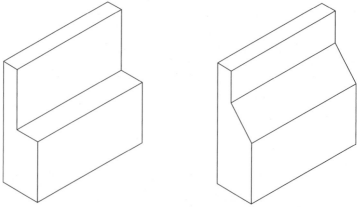

Figure 6-2: Changing a face thickness should be done with a transition.

All the materials used in injection molding shrink as they cool. Because parts freeze from the outside in, if there's a particularly large volume of material in a portion of the part, the cooling process may cause a portion of the exterior surface to become distorted and fall below the surrounding surface, which would give the appearance that a portion of the part is dented or has sunk. Designing consistent wall thickness and using walls instead of blocked off areas can improve quality and reduce problems caused by sink.

Radii

Sharp inside corners in a plastic part create stress concentrations where the part may eventually break. A properly designed injection-molded part has a radius at each interior corner. The CNC milling process may also leave a radius on outside corners of the part. Figure 6-3 illustrates the radii.

The size of the radius is important. It's helpful to have an interior radius that's equal to the wall thickness that it's connected to. Consistent wall thickness makes it easier for this rule of thumb to be applied.

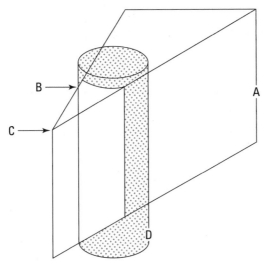

Figure 6-3: The radii on an injection-molded part.

See `http://www.protolabs.com/injection-molding/ fundamentals-of-molding` for additional information on injection molding design considerations.

Managing Injection Molding as Volume Demands Change

Good products will, theoretically, continue to grow in development, in market share, and in many cases, manufacturing volumes. For some companies, low- and mid-volume production in the tens of thousands is enough to carry their products from growth into maturity. Others will need a large-scale manufacturer (and likely steel tooling for injection molding) to reach the production capacity needed for market demand. When a product eventually summits at the peak of its life cycle, descending from the mountain can be equally challenging to manage. Instead of risky capital investments in high-volume manufacturing that can result in costly inventory expenses, on-demand or just-in-time (JIT) manufacturing is regularly used during a return to low-volume production as a product transitions into obsolescence.

The trajectory of a product isn't always as simple as a traditional bell-curve climb to a given height and back down again. Whether deliberately approached or unforeseen, there are peaks, valleys, and plateaus to negotiate along the way. Engaging with reliable manufacturing partners and using their injection molding capabilities appropriately can move you closer to product success.

Chapter 7

Ten Ways of Achieving Better Products with Proto Labs

. . . .

In This Chapter

▶ Getting what you need quickly

▶ Accessing the best technology

▶ Knowing part cost and design issues

▶ Having an extensive material selection

▶ Working with real engineers

▶ Getting the manufacturing services you need

▶ Having global access at your fingertips

▶ Making sure you can scale as needed

▶ Having resources to explore

▶ Getting top-quality production parts

. . . .

*T*his chapter provides ten reasons why working with the right digital manufacturing partner is so important.

Quick-Turn Manufacturing

These days, competitive market pressures dictate that you need to move quickly. Waiting around for weeks or months for parts to be produced means that you may miss the opportunity to get your product to market quickly enough to grab your fair market share.

Proto Labs has the capability to quickly manufacture the parts you need to bring your product to market much faster than traditional manufacturing processes typically allow. In many cases, Proto Labs can take your 3-D CAD model from idea to physical part in just a few days. This process is shown in Figure 7-1. Then, after you've had the chance to inspect, verify, and possibly modify the design, you can move to low-volume manufacturing with a process like injection molding.

Figure 7-1: The typical development process of moving a product from prototyping to production.

This quick turnaround from prototype to production may be just what's needed to get your product to market before your competitors.

With Proto Labs, you get:

- ✔ Injection-molded parts shipped in 1 to 15 days
- ✔ CNC-machined parts shipped in as fast as the day an order is placed
- ✔ 3-D-printed parts shipped in 1 to 3 days

Advanced Technology

Digital manufacturing has progressed significantly over the past decade, driven in large part by computing technology. When a 3-D CAD model is uploaded to Proto Labs, interactive quotes are sent back to you almost immediately, and when your part is ready to be made, digital instructions are sent to automated machinery that begin manufacturing your parts.

The technology behind this virtual interaction is complex software running on a massive compute cluster to help power both the quoting system and manufacturing. Using a company that embraces technological advancements in automation and manufacturing processes will typically help you achieve better, and faster, products.

One big advantage that Proto Labs has in technology is its sophisticated, dedicated, high-power computer systems that can quickly analyze your 3-D CAD models. These systems are specifically designed to produce fast results.

Automated Interactive Quoting

When you upload your 3-D CAD model to Proto Labs, its systems can quickly determine the cost to produce the parts and provide a design for manufacturability (DFM) analysis. Not only can you find out how much your parts would cost with various manufacturing processes, materials, and production volumes, but the analysis will highlight potential issues with your design before any actual manufacturing begins.

Because Proto Labs has the capability of producing parts in so many different ways, you're able to explore the best process to suit your needs. You typically receive an automated quote with pricing information and DFM analysis within 24 hours of uploading a 3-D CAD model. In some cases, Proto Labs even supplies a proposed revision of your CAD model with design changes already built in, which you can use if you so choose.

Range of Materials

Different parts call for different materials. In fact, the same part may even call for different materials as it moves from prototype to production part. You need a digital manufacturing partner with a range of materials and with the ability to suggest the best material for a given manufacturing process.

As mentioned in Chapter 3, the materials used in digital manufacturing can range from plastic and plasticlike materials to liquid silicone rubbers to metals. Some of these materials are specific to a particular manufacturing process, but others can be used (in slightly different forms) in more than one process.

Access to Live Engineering Expertise

No book or "how to" document can compare with the experienced eye of an expert or craftsman. It's all well and good to follow guidelines, but if you're not already experienced in digital manufacturing, you could be applying the wrong guidelines to your design.

You should work with people who can help you review your design and your needs. Experts can share information that may give you a different perspective on what rules apply to your specific situation. While Proto Labs' proprietary software does a lot of the initial design analysis, the human experts on staff can further guide the design for manufacturing.

Even if you have experience in manufacturing, Proto Labs' professionals can bring a fresh viewpoint to your situation and help you to see things in a new way. Digital manufacturing design processes and availability of materials are changing all the time, and people who think about these topics day and night are great people to have on your side.

Suite of Manufacturing Services

During the development timeline, production is often best served when much of the manufacturing can be handled in a single place — one company that truly allows you to take an idea from concept to thousands of parts within weeks.

Look for a manufacturer that has multiple in-house manufacturing processes like molding, machining, and 3-D printing, because each process serves a distinct purpose. One manufacturer brings added simplicity when moving from early prototyping to form, fit, and functional testing to short-run production that bridges the gap to large-scale manufacturing.

The versatility in manufacturing processes at Proto Labs lets you keep a significant amount, if not all, of your digital manufacturing at one service bureau. And if the time comes to jump elsewhere for large-scale production in the hundreds of thousands of parts, you have part designs that are ready.

Global Presence

For those who are looking for digital manufacturing outside of the United States, choosing a reliable company that has global experience is important. Proto Labs not only ships parts to many countries around the world, but also has production facilities in England and Japan to better serve its global base.

Scale of Operations

A manufacturing company with hundreds of machines and presses running at all times, day and night, means you're rarely told that your project is delayed due to capacity issues. It's a valuable capability that helps companies like Proto Labs turn your parts around within days, if needed. If you have multiple parts that need to be manufactured simultaneously, larger-scale facilities can also run those parts in parallel to further expedite the production process.

Proto Labs has the capability to manufacture parts as needed. Over a product's life cycle, you'll probably experience times when it simply doesn't make sense to stock a huge inventory of parts that may never be needed. By being able to get low-volume, on-demand parts, you're able to avoid production gaps without having to tie up capital in excess inventory.

Quality Parts

Nothing can doom a product's reputation as quickly as poorly made parts. You probably wouldn't think too highly of a modern smartphone with a shoddy back casing that kept falling off or of a luxury car that used cheap materials on the seats.

You need a digital manufacturing partner like Proto Labs that not only produces high-quality prototypes but engineering-grade production parts that can be used in end-use applications. First impressions do matter, and you simply can't afford to have your product make a bad impression because it doesn't say quality to the customer.

Extensive Resources

Find a digital manufacturing company that is willing to invest in building a library of educational resources for its customers. Proto Labs has created a comprehensive list of free content and materials for product designers and engineers to build the best products possible. These resources include the following:

- ✔ Physical design aids that explain injection molding and thermoplastic materials

- ✔ Detailed white papers that discuss topics like 3-D printing, LSR molding, MIM, and other complicated processes

- ✔ Design tips with advice on different design considerations for additive manufacturing, machining, and molding

- ✔ Regularly published Journal issues that cover industry trends, manufacturing advancements, and more

- ✔ Case studies that follow the development paths of products from every industry

- ✔ Entire *For Dummies* books that can be used as blueprints for digital manufacturing

Glossary

● ●

*H*ere's a quick list of manufacturing terms that may come in handy along your journey.

additive manufacturing/3-D printing: Commonly used interchangeably, additive manufacturing (3-D printing) involves a CAD model or scan of an object that is reproduced, layer by layer, as a physical three-dimensional object. Stereolithography, selective laser sintering, fused deposition modeling, and direct metal laser sintering are some of the commonly employed additive processes.

axial hole: A hole that's parallel to the axis of revolution of a turned part but doesn't need to be concentric to it.

bead blasting: Using glass beads or other abrasives in a pressurized air blast to create a surface texture on the part.

bevel: Also known as a *chamfer,* it is a flat truncated corner.

bridge tool: A temporary or interim mold for the purpose of making production parts until a high-volume production mold is ready.

brown part: The intermediate state of a MIM part after molding and debinding but before sintering. A brown part is porous and fragile, with just enough binder material remaining to keep the part from collapsing into a pile of powder.

build platform: The support base on an additive machine where parts are built. The maximum build size of a part is dependent on the size of a machine's build platform.

CAD: Computer-aided design.

catalytic debinding: The process of removing the binder from a green (as-molded) part by using a vaporized catalyst, resulting in a brown part.

chamfer: Also known as a *bevel,* it is a flat truncated corner.

cycle time: The time it takes to make one part in injection molding. This includes the closing of the mold, the injection of the resin, the solidification of the part, the opening of the mold, and the ejection of the part.

direct metal laser sintering: DMLS employs a laser system that draws onto a bed of metal powder, welding the powder into a solid. After each layer, a blade adds a fresh layer of powder and repeats the process until a final metal part is formed.

draft: A taper applied to the faces of an injection-molded part that prevents them from being parallel to the motion of the mold opening. This keeps the part from being damaged due to the scraping as the part is ejected out of the mold.

durometer: A measure of a material's hardness. It is often measured on a numeric scale ranging from lower (softer) to higher (harder). Shore A is one such scale.

ejection: The final stage of the injection molding process where the completed part is pushed from the mold using pins or other mechanisms.

end mill: A cutting tool that is used in CNC machining and other mills.

family mold: A mold where more than one cavity is cut into the mold to allow for multiple parts made of the same material to be formed in one cycle. Typically, each cavity forms a different part number.

feedstock: The raw material for metal injection molding, consisting of metal powder combined with a binder system. Feedstock in metal injection molding corresponds to resin in injection molding.

fillet: A curved face where a rib meets a wall, intended to improve the flow of material and eliminate mechanical stress concentrations on the finished part.

finish: A specific type of surface treatment applied to some or all faces of the part. This treatment can range from a smooth, polished finish to a highly contoured pattern that can obscure surface imperfections and create a better looking or better feeling part.

fully dense: In metal injection molding, fully dense generally corresponds to 96 to 99 percent density of a forged void-free, alloy-equivalent part.

fused deposition modeling: With FDM, coil of material in filament form is extruded from a print head into successive cross-sectional layers that harden into three-dimensional shapes.

green part: The intermediate state of a MIM part after molding and before debinding and sintering. A green part is soft and fragile compared to a typical injection-molded part, but is substantially stronger than a brown part.

initial graphics exchange specification (IGES): A common file format for exchanging CAD data.

injection: The act of forcing molten material into a mold to form a part.

layer thickness: The precise thickness of a single additive layer that can be as small as microns thin. Often, 3-D-printed parts will contain thousands of layers.

live tooling: Mill-like machining actions in a lathe where a rotating tool removes material from stock. This allows for the creation of features like flats, grooves, slots, and axial or radial holes within the lathe.

LSR: Liquid silicone rubber.

medical grade: Material that may be suitable for use in certain medical applications.

MIM: Metal injection molding.

net shape: The final desired shape of a part; or a shape that does not require additional shaping operations before use.

nozzle: The tapered fitting on the end of the barrel of an injection molding press where the resin enters the sprue.

on-axis hole: This is a hole that is concentric to the axis of revolution of a turned part. It is simply a hole on the end of a part and in the center.

parting line: The edge of a molded part where the mold separates.

porosity: Undesired voids included in a part. Porosity can manifest in many sizes and shapes from many causes. Generally, a porous part will be less strong than a fully dense part.

press: An injection molding machine.

radial hole: This is a hole formed by live tooling that is perpendicular to the axis of revolution of a turned part, and could be considered a side hole. The center line of these holes is not required to intersect the axis of revolution.

radiused: An edge or vertex that has been rounded.

resin: A generic name for chemical compounds that, when injected, form a thermoplastic part. Sometimes just called "plastic."

resolution: The level of printed detail achieved on parts built through additive manufacturing. Processes like stereolithography and direct metal laser sintering allow for extremely fine resolutions with the smallest of features.

selective laser sintering: During the SLS process, a CO_2 laser draws onto a hot bed of thermoplastic powder, where it sinters (fuses) the powder into a solid. After each layer, a roller lays a fresh layer of powder on top of the bed and the process repeats.

shrink: The change in part size as it cools during the molding process. This is anticipated based on material manufacturer recommendations and built into the mold design before manufacturing.

sink: Dimples or other distortion in the surface of the part as different areas of the part cool at different rates. These are most commonly caused by excessive material thickness.

sintering: The heating and condensing of a MIM part in a specialized furnace. MIM parts are sintered at temperatures nearly high enough to melt the entire metal part outright, at which the metal particle surfaces bind together to result in a final, 96 to 99 percent fully dense part.

STEP: *Standard for the Exchange of Product Model Data.* It is a common format for exchanging CAD data.

stereolithography: SL uses an ultraviolet laser focused to a small point to draw on the surface of a liquid photopolymer resin. Where it draws, the liquid turns to solid. This is repeated in thin, two-dimensional cross-sections that are layered to form complex three-dimensional parts.

sticking: A problem during the ejection phase of molding, where a part becomes lodged in one or the other half of the mold, making removal difficult. This is a common issue when the part is not designed with sufficient draft.

STL: Originally stood for "STereoLithography." It is a common file format for transmitting CAD data to additive manufacturing equipment and is not suitable for injection molding.

straight-pull mold: A mold that uses only two halves to form a cavity that resin is injected into. Generally, this term refers to molds with no side-actions or other special features used to resolve undercuts.

texture: A specific type of surface treatment applied to some or all faces of the part. This treatment can range from a smooth, polished finish to a highly contoured pattern that can obscure surface imperfections and create a better looking or better feeling part.

turning: During the turning process, rod stock is rotated in a lathe while a tool is held against the stock to remove material and create a radially symmetric part.

undercut: A portion of the part that shadows another portion of the part, creating an interlock between the part and one or both of the mold halves. An example is a hole perpendicular to the mold opening direction bored into the side of a part. An undercut prevents the part from being ejected, or the mold from opening, or both.

vent: A very small (0.001 in. to 0.005 in.) opening in a mold cavity, typically at the shutoff surface or via an ejector pin tunnel, that is used to let air escape from a mold while the resin is injected.

wall: A common term for the faces of a hollow part. Consistency in wall thickness is important.

warp: The curving or bending of a part as it cools that results from stresses as different portions of the part cool and shrink at different rates. Parts made using filled resins may also warp due to the way the fillers align during resin flow. Fillers often shrink at different rates than the matrix resin, and aligned fibers can introduce anisotropic stresses.

Notes

Notes